The Library of the Five Senses & the Sixth Sense™

Smell

Sue Hurwitz

The Rosen Publishing Group's
PowerKids Press™
New York

Published in 1997 by The Rosen Publishing Group, Inc.
29 East 21st Street, New York, NY 10010

First Edition

Book Design: Kim Sonsky

Photo Credits: Cover and all photo illustrations by Seth Dinnerman.

Hurwitz, Sue, 1934–
    Smell / by Sue Hurwitz.
        p.   cm. — (Library of the five senses & the sixth sense)
    Includes index.
    Summary: Explains the sense of smell, including how the nose works.
    ISBN 0-8239-5053-0
    1. Smell—Juvenile literature. [1. Smell. 2. Senses and sensation. 3. Nose.]
    I. Title. II. Series: Hurwitz, Sue, 1934– Library of the five senses (& the sixth sense)
QP458.H87 1997
612.8'6—dc21
                                                                        96–29964
                                                                            CIP
                                                                            AC

Manufactured in the United States of America

CONTENTS

Olivia

Olivia likes to play outside in her backyard. She smells many **odors** (OH-derz), or **scents** (SENTS), while she's there. She smells flowers and fresh grass. She smells burning leaves in the yard next door. She can smell gasoline from the gas station across the street.

There are good odors and bad odors. Fresh-baked cookies smell good. Skunks smell bad. When a skunk

4

gets frightened it sprays a bad-smelling liquid into the air. This is so people and other animals will stay away from the skunk.

Smells tell us about things that are good and things that could be bad for us.

Your Sense of Smell

Smelling is one of your **senses** (SEN-sez). Your senses tell you what is going on around you. Odors can tell you many things, such as what is near you or

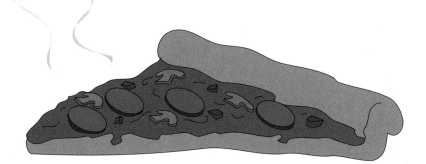

what is happening around you. Odors in a garden are different from odors at the pizza parlor.

Your sense of smell can also protect you. Odors can tell you when something is burning. Odors can warn you of rotten food that can make you sick.

Your Nose

Each person's nose looks different. The size and shape of your nose is sometimes like your parents' noses. The upper part of your nose is made of bone. This bony part protects the inside of your nose. The lower part of your nose is made of **cartilage** (KAR-til-ij). Cartilage is soft and rubbery.

Everybody's nose looks different!

9

Parts of Your Nose

Your nose has two openings called **nostrils** (NOS-trilz). Your nostrils have tiny hairs and small **blood vessels** (BLUD VES-elz). The nostrils lead to a hollow space called your **nasal cavity** (NAY-zul KA-vih-tee). The nasal cavity has bones and cartilage. It is lined with a sticky liquid called **mucus** (MYOO-kus). Mucus protects the inside of your nose from germs.

At the top of each nasal cavity is an **olfactory membrane** (ohl-FAK-toh-ree MEM-brayn). These are very small areas of skin inside your nose. The membranes have millions of tiny **nerve cells** (NERV SELZ). These cells help you smell.

10

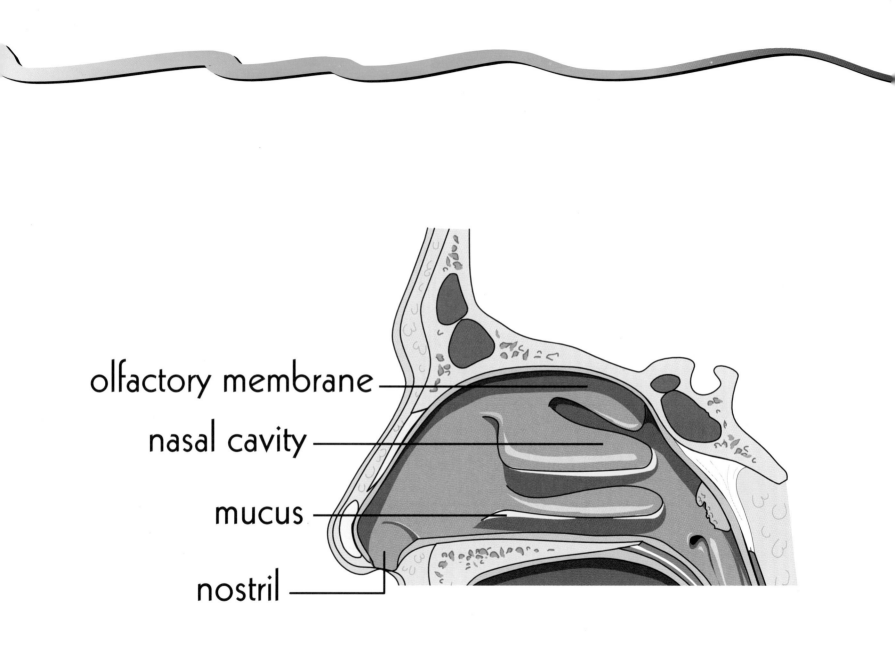

olfactory membrane

nasal cavity

mucus

nostril

How Do You Smell?

Scents travel into your nose with the air you breathe. The nerve cells in your nose tell your **brain** (BRAYN) what scents you are smelling. To smell something very well, you sniff. Sniffing pulls air and the scents in the air up to the top of your nose where your olfactory membranes are.

There are more than 10,000 different odors in the world. No one knows how many odors your nose can pick out. You usually smell more than one thing at a time. Things that have a scent send tiny odors into the air.

13

Smelling

The tiny odors from things that have a scent go to the nerve cells in your nose. You have fifteen kinds of nerve cells. They work together. These nerve cells help you pick out the many different odors around you. If you smell an odor just once, you will always be able to recognize it.

Some people have a better sense of smell than others. Sometimes our noses get used to the odors that are around us all the time and we stop noticing them.

You might smell a certain perfume that reminds you of one special person, such as a parent or a friend. ▶

Smelling and Your Brain

Odors mix with the mucus at the top of your nose. Each olfactory membrane connects to an **olfactory nerve** (ohl-FAK-toh-ree NERV). Each nerve sends a message to your brain. Your brain tells you what you're smelling.

People do not always like the same odors. Some people may like the scent of perfumes. Others may not. You probably will not like all the different scents around you.

YOUR NOSE AND BRAIN

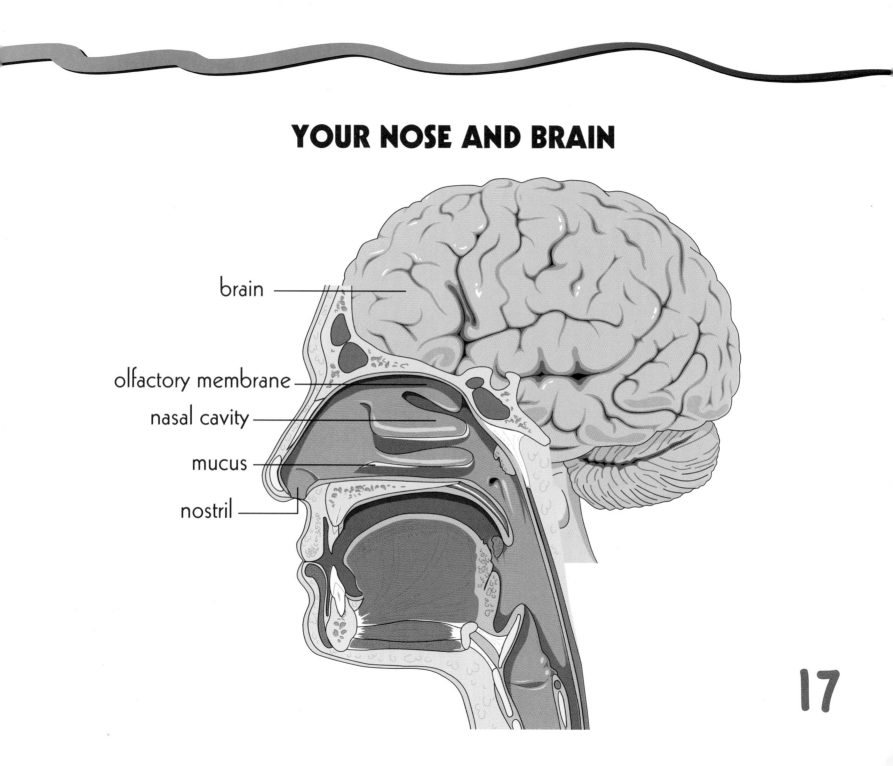

brain

olfactory membrane

nasal cavity

mucus

nostril

Smelling and Taste

Your nose, mouth, and throat are all connected inside your body. Your sense of smell is stronger than your sense of taste. The nerve cells in your nose help you taste the food in your mouth.

When you have a cold, the mucus in your nose gets thicker. The mucus clogs the nerve cells in your nose.

Then your sense of smell doesn't work as well. Your sense of taste also may not be as strong during a cold. And food may not taste as good.

Sneezing

When do you sneeze? You may smell a person's strong perfume. Or you may have a cold, and your nose is stuffy. Before you know it, you take a breath and "Ah-choo!" But why do you sneeze?

Sneezing can happen for different reasons. An odor or a tiny thing, such as dust, might go into your nostrils. Your nose knows that these things do not belong there. A sneeze pushes out the stuff that doesn't belong in your nose. You may also sneeze when your nose is full of mucus. Sneezing helps clear your nose.

21

Having a Healthy Nose

   You only have one nose, so it's important to take care of it. Remember these things:

- Cover your nose and mouth when you sneeze.
- Always blow your nose gently.
- Never put anything, including your fingers, into your nose.
- Protect your nose when playing sports. Wear safety **equipment** (ee-KWIP-ment).
- If your nose should bleed, gently squeeze the soft part of your nose. Hold it closed and ask a grown-up for help.

   Take care of your nose and it will take care of you—then you will be able to smell all of your favorite things!

22

Glossary

blood vessel (BLUD VES-el) A tiny tube in the body through which blood flows.

brain (BRAYN) The main nerve center in your head. The brain controls everything that your body does.

cartilage (KAR-til-ij) A soft but strong material that is found in many parts of your body.

equipment (ee-KWIP-ment) Tools or supplies a person uses to do something.

mucus (MYOO-kus) A thick liquid that lines your nose and other parts of your body.

nasal cavity (NAY-zul KA-vih-tee) A hollow space around which the bones and cartilage of your nose are located.

nerve cell (NERV SEL) A tiny, rope-like cell that sends messages to your brain about your body.

nostril (NOS-tril) An opening in your nose through which you breathe and smell.

odor (OH-der) A smell.

olfactory membrane (ohl-FAK-toh-ree MEM-brayn) A small area of skin in each nostril that has nerve cells that are used in smelling.

olfactory nerve (ohl-FAK-toh-ree NERV) One of two nerves that carry messages about what you smell from your nose to your brain.

scent (SENT) A smell.

senses (SEN-sez) The ways your body learns what is happening to you and the world around you.

23

Index